5 little shorties

Written and Illustrated by
Buist E. Hardison

ISBN 978-0-687-64150-5

07 08 09 10 11 12 13 14 15 16—10 9 8 7 6 5 4 3 2 1

Abingdon Press
Nashville

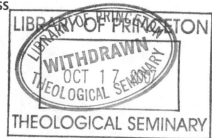

Five little Shorties all in a row
like beautiful flowers, how sweet they grow!
Five little Shorties,
Watch them jump!
Watch them spin!
Full of daddy's hugs and momma's kisses,
watch them chase the wind.

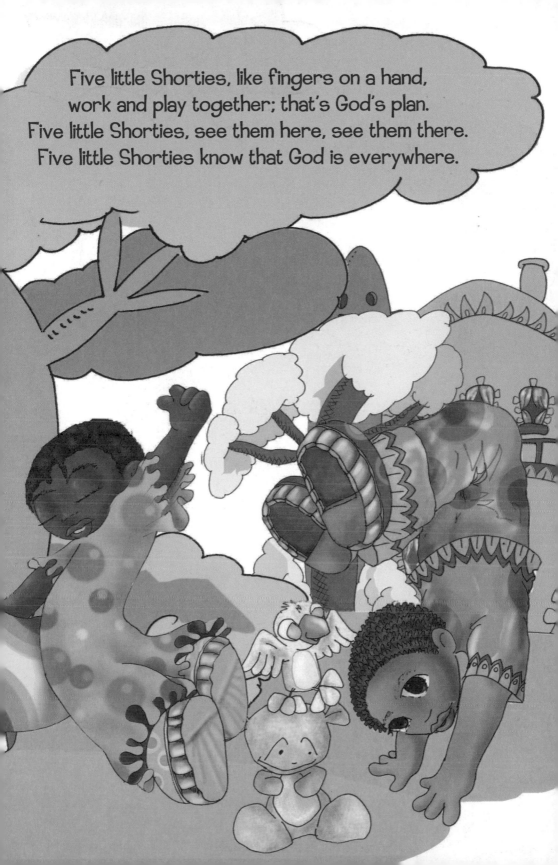

Little Shortie Dee is as
pretty as can be,
tells her Dolly stories
of a land far across the sea.

Little Shortie Dee is as cute as a kitten,
reads to her Dolly about kittens and lost mittens.

Little Shortie Dee never feels lost;
she knows God is always there.
Little Shortie Dee knows from the way
her momma braids her hair.

Little Shortie Eze with his drum,
he makes a racket.
Little Shortie Eze carries
around a noise basket.
Noise is his game.
Noise is his fame.
His mouth is never closed.
Shortie Eze is always bold.

Why is little Shortie Eze so loud and bold?
Shortie Eze knows that God is there.
Shortie Eze knows it
from the touch of the sun

as he runs.

but does not like to sit
to have her hair combed.

Little Shortie Nze has a turtle, Tag-a-long.
He's never fast or slow.
Just like Nze, he is always on the go.

Little Shortie Nze never feels alone
because little Shortie Nze knows that
God is always there.
Little Shortie Nze knows it when each
meal begins with prayer.

Little Shortie Tee has his two feet on the ground.
Little Shortie Tee with eyes so big and brown,
always looking for new things to do and see,
little Shortie Tee is as busy as a bee.

Little Shortie Tee has a bird called Mr. Beak.
Little Shortie Tee has a bear named Mr. Feet.
If you want to know why, just look at the size of his feet.
Little Shortie Tee knows God is there
because of all the wonder in this world to share.

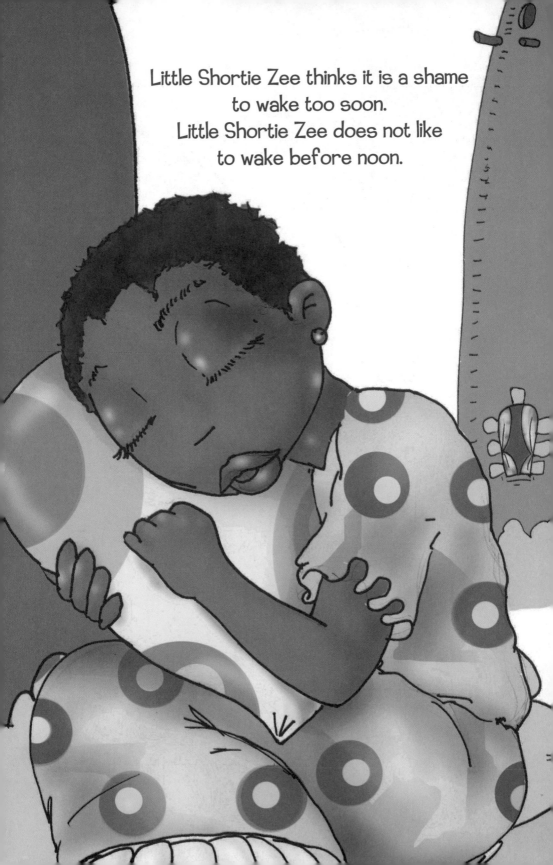

Little Shortie Zee thinks it is a shame
to wake too soon.
Little Shortie Zee does not like
to wake before noon.

Little Shortie Zee's eyes are never seen.
Perhaps she peeps,
but that's a secret she keeps.

Little Shortie Zee carries a pillow everywhere.
Little Shortie Zee is not afraid to take a dare.
How does she read and eat cake
with her eyes so closed?
Nobody knows.

Little Shortie Zee never wonders if
God is there.
Little Shortie Zee knows it from
the smell of flowers in the air.

Five little Shorties
all in a row
like beautiful flowers,
how sleepy Shorties grow!

How do little Shorties know
that God is there?
When they end each day
with a bedtime prayer.

Shortie Eze says good night, Drum;
our day is done.

Shortie Dee says good night, Dolly;
our day was fun.

Shortie Tee says good night,
Mr. Feet and Mr. Beak.

Shortie Zee says good night;
dreams are always sweet.